ESSENTIAL TIPS
101

AQUARIUM
FISH

ESSENTIAL TIPS

AQUARIUM
FISH

Dick Mills

DK PUBLISHING, INC.

www.dk.com

A DK PUBLISHING BOOK
www.dk.com

Editor Damien Moore
Art Editor Murdo Culver
DTP Designer Mark Bracey
Series Editor Charlotte Davies
Series Art Editor Clive Hayball
Production Controller Lauren Britton
US Editor Laaren Brown

First American Edition, 1996
10 9

Published in the United States by DK Publishing, Inc.,
95 Madison Avenue, New York, New York 10016

Visit us on the World Wide Web at http://www.dk.com

ISBN 0-7894-1074-5

Text film output by The Right Type, Great Britain
Reproduced in Singapore by Colourscan
Printed by Wing King Tong, Hong Kong

ESSENTIAL TIPS

PAGES 8-13

FISHKEEPING

1 ....Why keep fish?
2 ....Freshwater or marine?
3 ....Tropical freshwater
4 ....Coldwater freshwater
5 ....Tropical marine
6 ....Coldwater marine

PAGES 14-21

CHOOSING YOUR FISH

7 ....Specialty dealers
8 ......Four important considerations
9 ....Selecting hardy stock
10 ....What to look for in a fish
11 ....Unhealthy fish
12 ....Jetlagged stock
13 Considering the size of your fish
14 ....Compatible companions
15 ....Feisty fish
16 ....Filling the tank
17 ....Considering lifespans

PAGES 22-29

AQUARIUM EQUIPMENT

18 ....Getting started
19 ....Stocking levels
20 ....Tank shape
21 ....Siting your tank
22 ....The importance of filtration
23 ....Choosing a filter system
24 ....Biological filtration
25 ....The importance of aeration
26 ....Which air pump?
27 ....Heating the tank
28 ....Choosing a heater
29 ....Water supply
30 ....Using a sea mix
31 ....Water don'ts
32 ....Lighting for your aquarium

PAGES 44-49

HANDLING & HEALTH CARE

52 ....Observing your fish
53 ....Introducing new specimens
54 ....Catching fish
55 ....Prevent poisoning
56................................Cleaning tips
57.....................Changing the water
58...........................Stress-free travel
59..................Ailments & disorders
60.............................Hospital tanks
61...Clubs

PAGES 30-39

AQUASCAPING

33...............Setting up an aquarium
34............Tank-cleaning equipment
35 ....Base coverings for your tank
36....................Decorative materials
37 ....Starting your aquascape
38 ....The importance of plants
39.....Choosing plants for your tank
40 ....Artificial plants
41 ....The marine aquarium
42 ....Adding plants

PAGES 40-43

FEEDING YOUR FISH

43 ....Basic diet
44 ....Frequency of feeding
45 ....Choosing prepacked food
46 ....Choosing live foods
47 ....Culturing live foods
48 ....Food scraps
49 ....Food for all your fish
50................................Overfeeding
51................Vacation feeding needs

PAGES 50-57

TROPICAL FRESHWATER

62 ....Tiger barb
63 ....Zebra danio
64..White cloud mountain minnow
65 ....Red oscar
66 ....Siamese fighting fish
67 ....Black phantom tetra
68 ....Auratus
69 ....Angelfish
70 ....Striatum
71 ....Bearded corydoras
72 ....Swordtail
73 ....Dwarf chained loach
74 ....Discus
75 ....Guppy
76 .... Platy
77 ....Sailfin molly

PAGES 58-61

COLDWATER FRESHWATER

78 ....Common goldfish
79 ....Red shiner
80 ....Rudd
81 ....Moor
82 ....Bubble-eye goldfish
83 ....Shubunkin
84 ....Chinese sailfin sucker
85 ....Red & white ryukin

PAGES 62-67

TROPICAL MARINE

86 ....Flame angelfish
87 ....Jewel moray eel
88 ....Domino damselfish
89 ....Common clownfish
90 ....Copperbanded butterflyfish
91 ....Firefish
92 ....Crowned squirrelfish
93 ....Yellow tang
94 ....Longhorned cowfish
95 ....Mandarinfish
96 ....Cuban hogfish
97 ....Tailbar lionfish

PAGES 68-69

COLDWATER MARINE

98 ....Gunnel
99 ....Leopard-spotted goby
100 ....Fifteen-spined stickleback
101 ....Yarrell's blenny

INDEX 70
ACKNOWLEDGMENTS 72

FISHKEEPING

1 WHY KEEP FISH?

There are many advantages to keeping fish: they are relatively easy to take care of – routine maintenance only requires a few minutes daily, supplemented by an hour or so once a week; fish don't disrupt the home with messy fur or feathers; they don't need any exercise; and they don't make any noise. Anyone can keep fish, even in the smallest homes or in appartments where other pets are prohibited.

◁ ORNAMENTAL FISH
A well-maintained aquarium is an ornament to almost any home. Even if the fish themselves are relatively plain – as are these rainbowfish – a well-planted, well-lit tank is a joy to look at.

△ LOW-MAINTENANCE PETS
These handsome Tiger Barbs are hardy tropical freshwater fish that are easy to feed and relatively undemanding to keep.

◁ FASCINATING FISH
Learning about fish – their habits and habitats – is possibly the most fascinating aspect of fishkeeping.

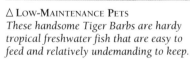

2 FRESHWATER OR MARINE?

To avoid disappointment, gain experience with freshwater fish before tackling the more demanding marine aquarium. Although tropical marine fish are undoubtedly the most spectacular species, many freshwater fish also display quite beautiful colors and long, elegant finnage. Freshwater tanks have the advantage of being able to support aquatic plants, which can make attractive features in their own right.

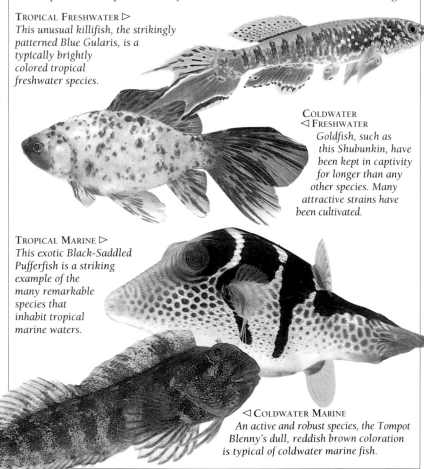

TROPICAL FRESHWATER ▷
This unusual killifish, the strikingly patterned Blue Gularis, is a typically brightly colored tropical freshwater species.

COLDWATER
◁ FRESHWATER
Goldfish, such as this Shubunkin, have been kept in captivity for longer than any other species. Many attractive strains have been cultivated.

TROPICAL MARINE ▷
This exotic Black-Saddled Pufferfish is a striking example of the many remarkable species that inhabit tropical marine waters.

◁ COLDWATER MARINE
An active and robust species, the Tompot Blenny's dull, reddish brown coloration is typical of coldwater marine fish.

3 TROPICAL FRESHWATER

The most popular branch of fishkeeping, the tropical freshwater system is also the easiest for the beginner, despite the fact that technical equipment is needed. The system supports a large range of species, most of which are relatively small and hardy. Tropical freshwater fish are often brightly colored. They require less space than fish from other systems.

△ SUNSET MARIGOLD HI-FIN PLATY
This bright orange platy is a cultivated variety of the grey-colored wild platy.

SIAMESE FIGHTING FISH ▷
When held erect in a show of aggression, the flowing fins of the male make a full circle on a perfect specimen.

STRIPED ANOSTOMUS △
This handsome, hardy species likes to feed among underwater roots and stout-leaved plants.

TROPICAL FRESHWATER AQUARIUM △
Bamboo and Giant Hygrophila provide the greenery in this attractive aquarium. Here, Tiger Barbs, Paradise Fish, and Gouramis thrive together.

◁ HEATER
A tropical freshwater aquarium must be kept heated to approximately 77°F (25°C).

4 COLDWATER FRESHWATER

This system does not require as much technology as its tropical counterpart, but it is more difficult to maintain. A more powerful filter is needed to keep the water clean and, because coldwater fish consume more oxygen than tropical types, a larger tank is necessary. Use aquatic plants to help oxygenate the water.

◁ FANTAIL GOLDFISH
As its name suggests, this Goldfish has a long, flowing twin caudal fin. The mottled coloration is variable.

BITTERLING △
This peaceful, schooling species has an attractive turquoise coloration, with clear fins.

RED-CAP ORANDA ▷
Like other fancy Goldfish, the Oranda should be kept in a tank free of active or aggressive fish.

Stems held erect by water

COLDWATER FRESHWATER AQUARIUM △
Common Goldfish and Comets stock this aquarium. A biological filter (see p.26) keeps the water clear and pure; aquatic plants help to oxygenate the water.

LUDWIGIA NATANS ▷

5 TROPICAL MARINE

This system has the highest initial cost because the fish are far more expensive than freshwater types. Once set up and stocked, running costs are not prohibitive, but be sure to get a year or two's experience with freshwater fish before moving on to this system; many tropical marine fish require special care.

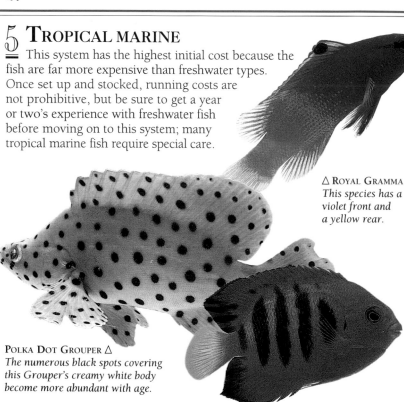

△ ROYAL GRAMMA
This species has a violet front and a yellow rear.

POLKA DOT GROUPER △
The numerous black spots covering this Grouper's creamy white body become more abundant with age.

△ FLAME ANGELFISH
Although relatively hardy and easy to manage, this fish can be territorial.

SEA ANEMONES ▽
Tropical anemones are often brightly colored and make an attractive addition to your aquarium.

△ TROPICAL MARINE COMMUNITY TANK
The tropical marine aquarium should be as large as possible for maximum water-quality stability. Provide plenty of hideaways and strong lighting.

6 COLDWATER MARINE

Because only a little equipment is required for this system and the fish can be collected for free, the coldwater marine aquarium can be inexpensive to set up and maintain. Although coldwater marine species tend to have dull coloring, their intriguing habits make them just as interesting as tropical fish. Many species quickly outgrow the tank and should be returned to the ocean.

LONG-SPINED SEA SCORPION ▷
This species can grow up to 10 in (25 cm) long. Despite its name and appearance, it is not poisonous.

◁ ROCK COCK
The Rock Cock is usually active during the day, but likes to rest among rocks at night.

FIFTEEN-SPINED STICKLEBACK ▷
This species has a distinctive spiny dorsal ridge. Sticklebacks require small live foods.

△ **COLDWATER MARINE AQUARIUM**
The mullets seen in this tank will eventually become too big for the tank. Stock your aquarium with crabs, anemones, starfish, and shrimps for added interest.

Seashells can be used as decorative material

SEASHELL

13

CHOOSING YOUR FISH

7 SPECIALTY DEALERS

Make sure that you buy your fish from a specialty fish dealer. This type of store will have a much wider choice of species than a local pet shop, and the fish will often be in better condition. Good dealers will take an interest in your needs and will offer sound advice on a range of fish and fish supplies.

MODERN OUTLET

8 FOUR IMPORTANT CONSIDERATIONS

Find out in advance which fish are suited to your aquarium, and establish whether any species will require special care (such as being fed live foods). Before buying your fish, take into account the following: aquarium suitability, physical health, ease of care, and compatibility with other fish.

A PRICKLY FISH ▷
Only very experienced fishkeepers should consider purchasing the venomous Tailbar Lionfish.

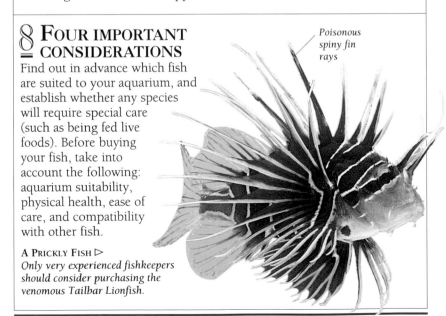

Poisonous spiny fin rays

⑨ SELECTING HARDY STOCK

Start off properly by picking the hardiest stock for your tank. This is most important if you are planning your first aquarium, because it will take time for you (and your fish) to become accustomed to your routine. Also, your fish must be hardy enough to survive any problems that may arise as a result of your lack of expertise. Do not be tempted by more exotic species that require expert handling until you have gained sufficient experience.

BUBBLE-EYE GOLDFISH △
The fluid-filled eye sacs are prone to damage.

△ SARASA COMET
A Comet is a very hardy coldwater freshwater fish.

SEA HORSES ▷
Although attractive, Sea Horses are difficult to keep.

△ HARLEQUIN RASBORA
Rasboras are attractive and undemanding fish, which enjoy the company of their own species.

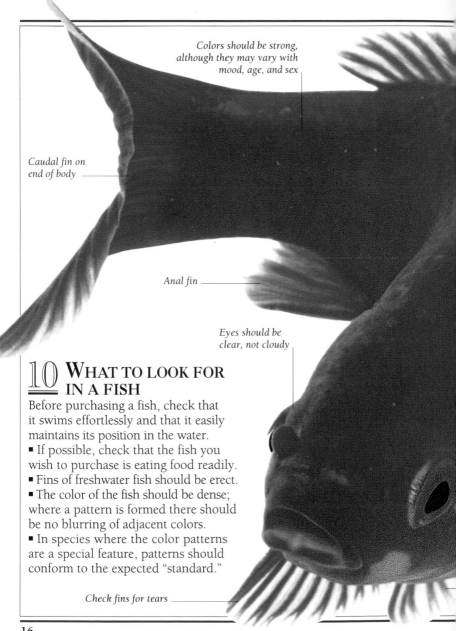

Colors should be strong, although they may vary with mood, age, and sex

Caudal fin on end of body

Anal fin

Eyes should be clear, not cloudy

10 WHAT TO LOOK FOR IN A FISH

Before purchasing a fish, check that it swims effortlessly and that it easily maintains its position in the water.
- If possible, check that the fish you wish to purchase is eating food readily.
- Fins of freshwater fish should be erect.
- The color of the fish should be dense; where a pattern is formed there should be no blurring of adjacent colors.
- In species where the color patterns are a special feature, patterns should conform to the expected "standard."

Check fins for tears

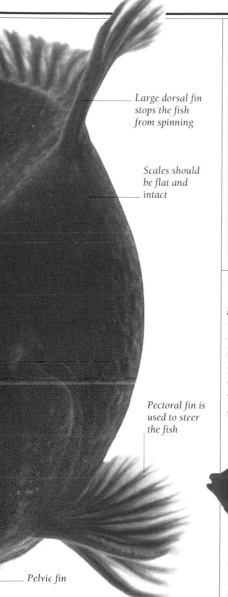

*Large dorsal fin
stops the fish
from spinning*

*Scales should
be flat and
intact*

*Pectoral fin is
used to steer
the fish*

Pelvic fin

11 UNHEALTHY FISH

The best way to avoid buying an unhealthy fish is to recognize the outward signs of illness.

■ Generally, avoid a fish that sulks in the corner of the tank, although it may be a species that is naturally shy.
■ An unhealthy fish may swim with its fins held flat against its body.
■ A fish suffering from an internal ailment may trail colorless excreta.
■ Don't choose a fish with boils, spots, lumps, open wounds, or split fins.
■ Never buy a fish from a tank that contains dead specimens.

12 JETLAGGED STOCK

A fish may have traveled for thousands of miles before reaching your local aquarist. A good dealer will often recommend that you do not buy new arrivals right away, as they may die from disease or stress. The dealer will be happy to reserve the fish for you until they are ready.

REGAL ANGELFISH
*This species naturally
inhabits Indo-Pacific reefs.*

13 CONSIDERING THE SIZE OF YOUR FISH

Always try to find out what adult, or maximum aquarium, size a fish will attain before you buy it. In the dealer's tank, the fish may appear to be just the size you want, but bear in mind that the fish are all juveniles, and their eventual size will be at least double their present size and possibly even larger. The fish shown here are similar in size as juveniles, but their adult sizes vary enormously. As a rule of thumb, remember that fish with big eyes or big scales usually turn out to be large.

△ COMMON GOLDFISH
The adult size of Goldfish is highly variable. Young fish may have a greenish bronze coloration.

△ RED-BELLIED PIRANHA
A notorious predator, this Piranha will grow up to about 12 in (30 cm) long.

FRENCH ANGELFISH △ ▷
Angelfish can grow to over 16 in (40 cm) long. Juvenile markings are often different from the adult's.

14 COMPATIBLE COMPANIONS

It is vital to select compatible fish for your aquarium. Many species naturally school and can become bored or aggressive if they are kept in a tank without another of their own species. On the other hand, some fish, although happy to share tank space with different species of fish, will not tolerate the company of their own species.

◁ BLACK-TAILED HUMBUG
Quarrels may occur between damselfish unless space and hideaways are provided.

▽ RED-STRIPED RASBORA
These little fish appreciate a well-planted aquarium with space for schooling.

15 FEISTY FISH

Be sure that you do not introduce a carnivorous fish into your aquarium or you will soon notice the disappearance of all your smaller fish. Any carnivorous species should be kept in a separate tank or in a communal aquarium with other species that are close in size.

Slender body with bright yellow fins

BLUE RIBBON EEL ▷
This predatory species must not be kept in a tank with smaller fish. It is territorial and needs plenty of rocky retreats.

16 FILLING THE TANK

To make full use of all of the space in your aquarium, select a range of species to occupy the different levels of the tank. Not all fish have the same habits; some are better adapted for feeding from the water surface, others cruise around in mid-water, while a third group rarely leaves the floor of the tank. By selecting fish from each of these levels, you can make full use of every bit of water depth in your tank.

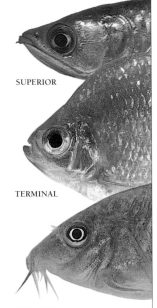

SUPERIOR

TERMINAL

INFERIOR

FISH MOUTH SHAPES ▷
The shape of a fish's mouth can provide a clue as to the tank level occupied by the species. Fish with superior mouths are surface feeders; a terminal mouth indicates a mid-water feeder; fish with inferior mouths feed on the bottom.

The upper level of the tank is relatively empty

Tetras are happy in all tank levels

TANK LEVELS
This tropical freshwater aquarium contains catfish, which are bottom-feeders, and tetras, which will feed at all levels of the tank.

Rams occupy the middle and lower tank levels

17 CONSIDERING LIFESPANS

When stocking your tank, it is worth considering the fact that not every fish lives to the same age. Coldwater freshwater fish tend to live the longest – some Koi and Goldfish live for over 20 years. Some species are naturally short-lived. Killifish, for example, may only live for a year. In general, the larger the fish, the longer it will live. Avoid buying fish with a humpbacked appearance uncharacteristic of the species. This deformity is a typical sign of old age.

Juvenile fish is dark blue with distinctive white markings

CHANGING COLOR
Young angelfish can be difficult to classify as they sometimes have remarkably different markings than adults.

JUVENILE ▷
EMPEROR ANGELFISH

Adult has diagonal yellow stripes on the body and a yellow tail

△ MATURE EMPEROR ANGELFISH

21

AQUARIUM EQUIPMENT

18 GETTING STARTED

Before you spend any money on fish for your aquarium, you must find out what equipment you will need to provide and maintain the environment that is essential for your fish's well-being. Investigate the various methods of heating, lighting, and cleaning your tank in advance.

SIEVE   BUCKET

LIGHTING HOOD

CLEANING EQUIPMENT △▷
You will need special equipment to make regular water changes and to keep your aquarium clean and clear if your fish are to remain healthy.

TANK

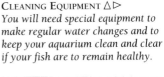

BIOLOGICAL FILTER PLATE

BIOLOGICAL POWER HEAD

TANK & LIGHTING △
Your ideal tank will depend largely on the type and number of fish that you intend to keep. Whichever tank you choose, be sure it has a cover and a built-in light.

FILTERS, HEATERS, & PUMPS △▷
An electric pump and filter is required to help keep the tank water clean and fresh. If you wish to keep tropical fish, you will need to purchase a heater.

SYPHON

PLATE

SPONGE

NET

SCRUB BRUSH

SCISSORS

THERMOMETER

CABLE
CADDY

HEATER

EXTERNAL
POWER FILTER

19 STOCKING LEVELS

It is important to calculate the number of fish that your tank can support, bearing in mind that the oxygen consumption of the main fish groups (see p.11) differs. Overstocking a tank can, quite literally, suffocate your fish.

TROPICAL FRESHWATER: FOUR CATFISH

COLD FRESHWATER: TWO GOLDFISH

TROPICAL MARINE: ONE ANGELFISH

TAKING STOCK
A tank measuring 24 in (60 cm) long by 12 in (30 cm) wide with a surface area of 288 in² (1,800 cm²) will support four 6 in (15 cm) catfish, two 4½ in (11.5 cm) Goldfish, or one 6in (15 cm) marine angelfish.

20 TANK SHAPE

You can have any shape tank you like, bearing in mind that the number of fish in the aquarium depends on the surface area, *not* the depth, or the overall volume of water. The two tanks shown here contain the same volume of water, but because the upright tank has a smaller surface area of water compared with the horizontal tank, it will support fewer fish. The "standard" tank shape is based on the double cube, with the longest side being the horizontal.

Same volume of water as horizontal tank

Greater surface area than upright tank

Lower oxygen level means fewer fish

UPRIGHT △ TANK

Higher oxygen level supports many more fish

◁ HORIZONTAL TANK

21 SITING YOUR TANK

Make sure that you choose a suitable position for your aquarium on a very firm, level base, away from cold drafts and direct sunlight.
- Avoid window locations; too much sunlight will cause overheating, and excessive algae growth will result.
- Site your tank near an electrical socket point to provide power to run airpumps, heaters, and filters.
- Cushion the tank with a slab of expanded polystyrene to absorb any irregularities in the surface below.
- Leave enough space around the tank for all hardware, and to allow access for aquarium maintenance.
- Never attempt to move a full tank, not even to reposition it slightly.

22 THE IMPORTANCE OF FILTRATION

It is absolutely essential that the water in the aquarium stays clean and fresh at all times if your fish are to remain healthy. No matter how attractive your aquarium appears when you first set it up, the water will quickly become contaminated by dissolved waste products from the fish. This dirt, whether visible or not, can be removed by using a filter. However, remember that the filter itself needs to be properly maintained because a neglected filter becomes nothing more than a box of concentrated dirt through which the aquarium water is continually passed. Water returning from filters helps oxygenate the aquarium.

Pump for undergravel filter system

Plant leaves are bright green

Tank water is clear

Fish are healthy and active, with dense colors

FILTER IN TANK

23 CHOOSING A FILTER SYSTEM

◁ INTERNAL FILTER ▷

◁ EXTERNAL FILTER

Filtration equipment varies from simple foam filters to sophisticated "total" filter systems. An external, air-operated filter has several advantages: it is inexpensive, efficient, and easy to access and clean. Internal filters, although often simple and effective, have a major drawback – cleaning and maintenance is difficult, and as the filter is removed, dirty water can spill back into the tank. Biological filtration (*see p.26*) is an effective system that works without a filter medium.

24 BIOLOGICAL FILTRATION

This filtration system, which has no filter medium, introduces a colony of beneficial bacteria into the gravel surface in order to neutralize toxic substances in the water. It has several advantages over other types of filter. It is relatively unobtrusive, needs no long hoses, and is quiet in operation. Suitable for all aquariums, it is obligatory for marine systems.

Power head pulls water through gravel

TANK WITH BIOLOGICAL FILTER

Bacterial colony lives on gravel surface

Water drawn through slotted plastic plates

25 THE IMPORTANCE OF AERATION

Not only does the water need to be clean; it must also contain a healthy amount of oxygen. This is especially important in coldwater aquariums during the summer months, when the dissolved oxygen level falls as the water warms up. An air pump is an artificial aid that introduces more oxygen into the water and, at the same time, disperses some of the harmful carbon dioxide. Aeration has another advantage in that it helps to equalize the temperature throughout the aquarium.

26 WHICH AIR PUMP?

The larger the pump, the more air it produces. However, even the smallest air pump will provide enough air for a standard-sized tank. You will need a large air pump only if you intend to use it for purposes other than simple aeration, such as to operate filters, airstones, or brine-shrimp hatchers.

Air to tank nozzle

◁ AIR PUMP

27 HEATING THE TANK

Unlike other aquarium hardware, such as lights, air pumps, and filters, heaters are only necessary if you want to keep tropical species. Use a thermostatically controlled heater to maintain the water temperature at around 77°F (25°C). Some have alarms to alert owners to changes.

TROPICAL FISH △▷
If all other conditions are satisfactory, tropical species, such as these extraordinary Discus, will thrive in an aquarium where the temperature is maintained at a constant of about 77°F (25°C).

DO NOT OVERHEAT
A large heater in a small tank will work normally, but if the thermostat malfunctions it will quickly overheat the water.

Suction pad fixes thermometer to glass

HEATER ▷
WITH
THERMOSTAT

△ INTERNAL THERMOMETER

86 84 82 81 79 77 75 73 72 70 68 66 °F
30 29 28 27 26 25 24 23 22 21 20 19 °C

△ EXTERNAL THERMOMETER

28 CHOOSING A HEATER

The heater you choose for your tank must be powerful enough to heat it properly. As a guide, allow 10 watts of power per gallon of water for a tank that is in a normally heated room. For tanks over 36 in (90 cm), heat distribution is more even if you spread the heater requirement over two separate units.

29 WATER SUPPLY

It is always the best policy to give your fish water that is as close as possible in quality to that in which they are found naturally. However, the majority of aquarium fish adjust well to domestic water supplies, provided that precautions are taken to neutralize the effects of any chemicals that may be added.

HARD-WATER FISH ▷
*Certain fishes, such as this
Lemon Cichlid, thrive best
in hard water.*

◁ SOFT-WATER FISH
*Many species, like this Ram,
are naturally adapted
to a soft-water habitat.*

30 USING A SEA MIX

If you live near the coast, you will have access to a ready supply of natural seawater for your marine aquarium. However, it is usually better to use a synthetic substitute, known as a "sea mix," to avoid the risk of introducing disease. Mixes are available in different-sized bags to suit different tank sizes.

SEA-SALT
◁ MIX

31 WATER DON'TS

- Don't make any sudden changes in the water conditions.
- Do not change the water in the tank unless it is the correct composition and temperature.
- Don't change fish from tank to tank unless the water condition in each of the tanks is exactly the same.
- Don't use saltwater to top off evaporation losses in marine tanks, use freshwater instead as salts are not lost during evaporation.
- If you use rainwater in your tank, don't collect it from a dirty roof or from metallic containers.
- Water and electricity do not mix.

32 LIGHTING FOR YOUR AQUARIUM

Besides allowing you to see the contents of your aquarium properly, light acts as a stimulus for life, both for fish and plants. Plants require the right amount of light in order to photosynthesize.

This action is beneficial to fish since it keeps carbon dioxide levels down to a minimum. Use fluorescent rather than tungsten lighting, which produces uneven illumination and excessive heat.

COMMON MISTAKE
Don't follow the common practice of lining the tank hood with metal cooking foil as the foil will block the ventilation holes through which unwanted carbon dioxide and heat escape.

White reflector hood

Fluorescent tube

△ LIGHTING HOOD

LIGHTING CONTROLLER
Dimmer switches and timers can be used to regulate the intensity and duration of light in your aquarium.

Bogwood provides shelter for nocturnal species

Shadows are cast behind fish

Plants thrive under strong lighting

ILLUMINATED AQUARIUM
In this tropical freshwater aquarium the lighting is mounted in the hood so that light is reflected slightly toward the rear of the tank, accentuating the fish's natural iridescences.

AQUASCAPING

33 SETTING UP AN AQUARIUM

Aquascape your aquarium using materials such as gravel, rocks, driftwood, and plants to make it attractive as well as functional. However, your main priority should be to establish a safe and healthy environment for your fish. Try to simulate the natural habitat of your chosen species and select your plants and other decorative materials accordingly. Use rocks and plants to create plenty of hiding places for the more timid species.

PEA GRAVEL ▷

BASE MATERIAL
Pea gravel and other base materials provide a growing medium for many aquarium plants.

Driftwood helps conceal the heater and filter

Water wisteria provides shelter for timid fishes

Taller plants are placed in the background

TROPICAL FRESHWATER COMMUNITY AQUARIUM
A community aquarium such as this brings together a range of fish and plants that will thrive together even though they originate from different habitats.

A Java Fern is positioned in the foreground

⊲ROCKS

⊲DRIFTWOOD

DECORATIVE MATERIAL
*Materials such as rocks or
driftwood are particularly
useful for hiding unsightly
technical equipment.*

△ DWARF
SWORDPLANT

⊲HAIRGRASS

JAVA FERN △

WATER WISTERIA ▷

PLANT MATERIAL
*In freshwater aquariums,
plants provide a source of
food and oxygen as well as
being highly decorative.*

△ CONGO
ANUBIAS

34 TANK-CLEANING EQUIPMENT

Whatever materials you use for
aquascaping your tank, they must
always be thoroughly cleaned and
free from all foreign matter. It is
worth purchasing special cleaning
equipment: a sieve to wash gravel;
a bucket to wash plants and soak
bogwood; and a scouring pad or
brush to scrub rocks. Thoroughly
clean any plants that you wish to
use in your aquarium in order to
avoid the risk of introducing
parasites or predators.

*A sieve is useful for
cleaning gravel*

CLEANING WOOD
*Soak bogwood in a
bucket of water. Replace dirty water at
regular intervals until it remains clear.*

35 BASE COVERINGS FOR YOUR TANK

Pea gravel with a particle size of around ⅛ in (3 mm) is ideal for most freshwater tanks. Other materials, such as aquarium peat and coal, are also available if you wish to simulate a specific habitat. Sand or pebbles collected from the seashore are suitable materials for marine tanks. Crushed coral sand is also an option, but it is expensive.

PEA GRAVEL

AQUARIUM PEAT

COAL-GRAVEL MIX

RED GRAVEL

AQUARIUM SOIL

COAL

NATURAL SHADES
Avoid using artificially colored gravel in your aquarium: the glaring colors will detract from the coloration of your fishes, and dyes may escape and adversely affect the chemistry of the water.

SILVER SAND

CORAL SAND

36 DECORATIVE MATERIALS

Enhance your aquascape and conceal unsightly hardware with rocks, shells, and logs. However, take care that you do not obstruct the filter pipes. Attach wood to bits of slate using sealant, to prevent it from floating to the surface.

△ SEA SHELLS

△ STRATIFIED ROCK

SHALE ▷

△ SNAIL SHELLS

DECORATIVE SHELLS
Shells can enhance the look of your tank. Position larger shells carefully so small fishes cannot enter them and become trapped.

△ IGNEOUS ROCK

MARBLE ▷

BEDS OF ROCK
Rocks can be used to create banks and "cliff faces." For the fishes' safety, avoid rocks with sharp edges.

△ SMALL STONES

◁ IMITATION WOOD

UNDERWATER WOOD △▷
Use branches to simulate tree roots. Pieces of wood will look like sunken logs if they are positioned carefully.

△ DRIFTWOOD

37 STARTING YOUR AQUASCAPE

The key to setting up your aquarium successfully is to plan everything thoroughly beforehand. Not only do the fish need to be compatible, but everything that goes into the tank, including rocks and plants, must be suited to the system you have chosen. Planning your aquascape on paper before you begin will save you both time and money in the long run. A good design should hide technical hardware, while leaving plenty of space for the fish to swim freely.

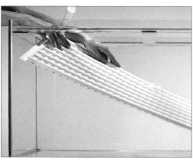

1 When using a biological filtration system (*see p.26*), the undergravel filter plate must be maneuvered into position before adding your base.

2 Pour your base material across the bed of the tank. Create a slope at a ratio of 1:5 from front to back to give the aquarium a sense of perspective.

3 Strategically position a range of rocks, to hide aquarium hardware and to provide hiding places for the more reclusive species of fish.

4 Add driftwood to enliven your design. Make sure that each piece of wood is weighed down or pushed deep into the gravel so it does not float to the surface.

38 THE IMPORTANCE OF PLANTS

Aquatic plants will visually enhance your freshwater tank and give fish shade and shelter.

- Plants keep the water conditions pure by absorbing carbon dioxide and giving off oxygen.
- Aquatic plants also help remove another waste product: nitrate. If you have a biological filter installed in your aquarium, this will break down ammonia (which fish excrete) into less harmful nitrate, which aquatic plants are then able to utilize as food.
- For a healthy aquarium, ensure your plants receive plenty of light.

FISH CAMOUFLAGE △
Some fish appreciate the shelter provided by aquatic plants. This Blockhead Cichlid rests secure, camouflaged among dense aquatic vegetation.

Its distinctive stripes allow the Zebra Loach to hide among vegetation

△ ZEBRA LOACH

VEGETARIAN FISH ▷
Aquatic plants provide an important part of the diet of many fish. This omnivorous Silver Dollar Tetra enjoys eating soft-leaved plants.

SILVER DOLLAR TETRA ▷

39 CHOOSING PLANTS FOR YOUR TANK

Not only do your fish need to be compatible, plants must also be suited to the particular system that you have chosen. Some genera contain both coldwater and tropical species, but this does not mean that every species within these genera can be used in both systems. Some coldwater types, however, can be acclimatized to tropical conditions.

◁ BAMBOO PLANT

△ DWARF ANUBIAS

TROPICAL PLANTS △▷
An enormous range of tropical plants is now available to fishkeepers. Check that the ones you choose are healthy and easy to care for.

GIANT △ HYGROPHILA

◁ GIANT RED ROTALA

EEL GRASS ▷

△ WATER STAR

◁ WATERWEED

◁ △ COLDWATER PLANTS
Coldwater plants can be collected from local ponds and streams, but they must be cleaned thoroughly before use.

40 ARTIFICIAL PLANTS

If you keep herbivorous fish species, they will quickly denude your tank of any plants. Artificial replicas are available as inexpensive alternatives. Made of supple plastic in a variety of colors, they have a base-plate that you must bury firmly in the gravel at the bottom of the tank.

ARTIFICIAL SEAWEED △▷

41 THE MARINE AQUARIUM

Live plants cannot be kept in a marine aquarium, but you can add synthetic plants (see above) and corals to enhance your tank. Sea anemones are suitable for both tropical and coldwater systems. Macro-algae, which make an excellent source of food for many species of fish, are also available. Algae growth can become rampant under strong light, however, and will obscure the tank if left unchecked.

◁ TROPICAL MARINE HABITAT
All green "plants" found in tropical marine aquariums are, in fact, macro-algae, which can become rampant.

42 ADDING PLANTS

When planting your aquarium, begin by placing taller species around the back and sides of the tank. But don't hide the glass completely – by leaving small gaps you will create the illusion of space beyond. Low-growing species look particularly good in front of rocks and caves. Select a "star" specimen plant, which stands out from the rest of the plants, as a centerpiece for your aquascape.

AVOID BLOCKING THE LIGHT
Plants that float freely on the surface of the water should be used sparingly. They tend to run rampant and can block out the light needed by other species.

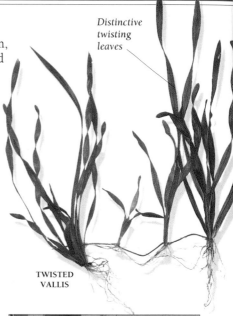

Distinctive twisting leaves

TWISTED VALLIS

1 It is advisable to add water before you begin planting, so that you can immediately judge the effect of your efforts. Run the water over the rocks to avoid disturbing the base. Do not fill the tank completely until you finish planting.

2 Begin by placing tall plants around the back and sides of the tank. Do not push the plants too deeply into the gravel – the crown should be level with or just above the gravel bed. Spread the plant's roots out in the gravel.

3 To maintain a natural look, plant each species in groups. The Hairgrass, shown here, effectively hides the filter intake tube and will provide a welcome retreat for shy fish or harassed females.

4 Once you have built a backdrop of tall plants, use medium-sized, bushy plants as space fillers, and place smaller species in the foreground. Finally, add your specimen plant as a centerpiece.

This large-leaved Anubias makes a fine specimen plant

Water wisteria has an attractive ragged texture

Twisted vallis has been used to hide the intake tube

FINISHED AQUASCAPED TANK
The finished aquascape successfully hides the technical hardware and provides plenty of hiding places for the fish. The plants, branches, rocks, and gravel display an interesting variety of textures and shades.

A Java Fern adds interest to the foreground area

FEEDING YOUR FISH

43 BASIC DIET

Like other vertebrates, fish need carbohydrates, minerals, vitamins, fats, proteins, and water. The best way to give your fish all the nutrients they require is to feed them a varied diet of good-quality foods, including live food as well as manufactured food.

FEEDING REGIME
In a community tank, flakes will feed the surface feeders, pellets the bottom feeders, and live foods the mid-water feeders (see p.20).

44 FREQUENCY OF FEEDING

Feeding fish "little and often" is preferable to providing them with one large daily meal. Add small amounts of food two or three times a day, and try to vary each meal so that your fish don't become bored with their diet. If other members of your family also look after the aquarium, make sure that you have set feeding times, or that everyone knows when the fish have just been fed, so that you do not overfeed them between you.

GOLDFISH ▷
RISING TO FEED

45 CHOOSING PREPACKED FOOD

Make sure you buy some all-in-one, "complete," dried fish food, which contains everything your fish need to remain healthy.

Flakes are ideal for smaller fish as they can be crumbled into tiny portions. Specialized foods are available for single-species tanks.

FLAKE FOOD ▷
Flake food is the best all-in-one dried fish food. It tends to float for a while, so feeding surface feeders; it then sinks slowly, and is swallowed by mid-water feeders; finally, bottom feeders clean up the flakes missed by the other fish.

△ "SPECIALIZED" FLAKE FOOD

"COMPLETE" FLAKE FOOD △

◁ PELLETS & TABLETS
Pellets, granules, and tablets, which usually sink quickly, are ideal for bottom-feeding fish. Stick tablets onto the glass for mid-water feeders.

△ PELLETS

△ TABLETS

FREEZE-DRIED SHRIMPS △

◁△ FROZEN FOODS
Freshly caught natural foods that have been frozen for storage can be fed to fish at a later date, with no degradation of their food value.

△ FREEZE-DRIED TUBIFEX WORMS

FROZEN BLOODWORM △

46 CHOOSING LIVE FOODS

Give your fish live food as a treat. Fish derive a good deal of nutritional benefit from live food, and they visibly enjoy hunting the insects that you introduce into the aquarium. Brine shrimp, bloodworms, and waterfleas are available from many aquatic dealers. Or collect specimens from your garden or a local pond.

△ WATER FLEAS

△ BRINE SHRIMP

◁ TUBIFEX WORMS   △ BLOODWORM

INTRODUCING PREDATORS
Many insects found in ponds are predatory to smaller fish and should not be introduced into your tank. These include dragonfly larvae and leeches.

47 CULTURING LIVE FOODS

Small worms can be cultured to provide a disease-free, year-round supply of live food. Begin by buying a culture of whiteworm from your dealer. Place the worms in a box of earth or compost and place a slice of wet bread on the top for the worms to feed on. They should breed rapidly and provide you with a continuous supply of fish food. Alternatively, you can culture brine shrimps by hatching storebought eggs in a warm saltwater solution (1 tsp of sea salt to 1 quart of tap water).

48 FOOD SCRAPS

Much of the food that we eat ourselves is suitable for fish when served in appropriately scaled-down portions. Slivers of meat, crumbled cheese, shredded lettuce or spinach leaves, canned peas, wheat germ, and oat flakes are all acceptable items.

◁ PEAS

LETTUCE LEAVES ▷

49 FOOD FOR ALL YOUR FISH

If you have a community aquarium, you will find that it is not practical to make up a meal containing small amounts of the different foods for each species, so the best thing to do is to feed tablets at one meal, flake at another, live food at another, and so on.

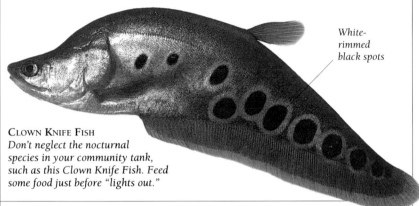

White-rimmed black spots

CLOWN KNIFE FISH
Don't neglect the nocturnal species in your community tank, such as this Clown Knife Fish. Feed some food just before "lights out."

Pinch food between thumb and forefinger

50 OVERFEEDING

Feed your fish sparingly as any uneaten food will decompose in the tank and eventually cause pollution problems. A good method for measuring out the right amount of food for one meal is to give as much as you can pinch between your thumb and forefinger.

51 VACATION FEEDING NEEDS

As long as your fish are well fed before your vacation, they will be able to withstand a two-week fast without any ill effects. If, however, you prefer to ask a friend to feed your fish, make up several small packages of fish food in the correct amount for one serving and leave instructions for the serving times for each of the packs.

- Automatic feeders are available at greater expense.

HANDLING & HEALTH CARE

52 OBSERVING YOUR FISH

Take every opportunity to watch your fish and get to know the behavior patterns of each species. A regular observation routine will help you in two ways: you will spot immediately if any fish are sick, and you will be aware of any tasks that need to be done to keep your aquarium in good condition.

■ Begin by checking regularly that all your fish are present. Don't panic, however, the first time you can't see all your fish. Timid species can hide themselves very effectively.

■ Watch out for aggressive traits, such as fin-nipping, but remember that some fish will behave this way out of loneliness if deprived of the companionship of their own species.

UNUSUAL HABIT △
The Twinspot Wrasse, with its distinctive false "eyes," burrows in the sand to evade enemies.

LOACHES ON THE BED ▽
Most fish rest by remaining still for several hours at a time. These bottom-dwelling Clown Loaches like to rest on the gravel bed.

53 INTRODUCING NEW SPECIMENS

Stress, which can lead to disease or death, is caused by bad handling or inconsiderate treatment, so it is very important to develop a gentle but effective technique when handling your fish. When you purchase new fish, add them to your tank very carefully, as shown here. There will probably be a notable difference in temperature between the water in the fish's bag and that in the tank, and any such sudden change may stress the fish. When introducing marine fish into a new tank, you should switch the aquarium lights off, but leave the room lights on.

1 △ Float a plastic bag containing the new fish in the aquarium for 10–15 minutes, until the water in the bag reaches the same temperature as the tank water.

2 △ Open the bag and gently coax the fish out with a net. Avoid pouring too much water from the bag into the tank, as it may contain harmful bacteria.

3 △ Tip the net gently – take care to avoid trapping the fish's fins in the netting. Allow the fish to swim into the tank in their own time.

54 CATCHING FISH

Netting is always a terrifying experience for fish, so it is crucial to develop a gentle netting technique. When using a single net, keep it constantly on the move. Using two nets will help speed up the process. Keep one net moving, and hold the other, which must be larger than the fish you are catching, stationary in the fish's path. If you do not have a net, you can use a transparent plastic bag to catch your fish.

Hold the larger net stationary in the fish's path

Use a small net to encourage the fish into the larger one

LARGE NET

SMALL NET

CATCHING FISH USING TWO NETS

55 PREVENT POISONING

You must exercise strict control over everything that you put into your aquarium. To avoid poisoning your fish, don't let any metal get into the water, especially in marine aquariums, where even condensation dripping back from a metal hood will contaminate the water. Cover any metal fittings (such as external thermostat clips) with tubing in order to prevent contact with the water. Avoid using internal thermostat or heater units that have metal attachments.

56 CLEANING TIPS

For your fish to thrive and your tank to look attractive, you must carry out certain routine cleaning tasks. Keeping the tank clean allows light to reach the plants. Remember to remove dead leaves and scrape away excess algae. Clean the filter as necessary.

1 ▽ Switch off the lighting, filter, and heater. Wipe the condensation tray, if you have one, with a damp sponge.

2 ▽ Prune your plants with scissors. Cuttings can be replanted to provide new specimens.

3 ▽ Remove excess algae with a scraper. Leave some algae at the back of the tank for your fish to feed on.

4 ◁ Clean the filter casing thoroughly. Remove the filter medium and wash out any dirt using water taken from your tank. Replace the filter medium if necessary.

Clean filter sponges in old tank water

57 CHANGING THE WATER

Although an efficient filter will do much to maintain the water quality (*see p.25*), help keep your aquarium clean by making regular, partial water changes. In a freshwater system, replacement of about 20 percent of the water every 3–4 weeks is recommended; in a marine aquarium you should change 25 percent of the water every 2–3 weeks. Always use "sea-mix" when changing water in marine tanks.

1 Siphon about one fifth of the aquarium water into a bucket. Move your siphon around the front of the tank where unsightly detritus collects.

2 Condition tap water to refill your tank. In a marine aquarium you must use "sea-mix" in order to maintain the correct water density.

3 With the new water at the right temperature, refill your aquarium. Pour the water carefully over a plate, to avoid disturbing your fish.

58 STRESS-FREE TRAVEL

Transporting your fish (whether from the dealer's to your home, to the vet, or to fish shows) is a potentially stressful experience for them. Carrying fish in a plastic bag is perfectly acceptable in the summer, or for short journeys, but in colder weather, or for longer trips, it is worth obtaining an insulated transportation box.

Clear plastic bag

Goldfish

59 AILMENTS & DISORDERS

It is crucial to detect disease in your fish as early as possible. Prompt treatment may save the afflicted fish, and, perhaps even more importantly, prevent the disease from spreading to your other fish.

- When inspecting your fish, look for any physical changes, such as the appearance of abnormal growths, changes in the body shape or scales, or damage to the fins.
- Check if any fish are having trouble swimming. Swimming difficulties may indicate a swim-bladder disorder.
- Check for the presence of parasites.

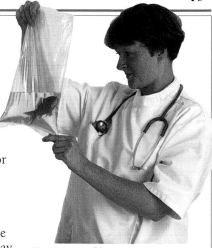

VISITING THE VET
If in doubt, pay a visit to your local vet for advice on the health of your fish.

A HEATED HOSPITAL TANK

60 HOSPITAL TANKS

Keep a small tank for the treatment of sick fish and for quarantining new arrivals. Create a reassuring environment in the tank using plastic plants – real ones are killed by fish medications – and a hideaway. Between treatments, always thoroughly disinfect the tank and any equipment used in it.

61 CLUBS

If you want to become more involved in your hobby, ask at your local fish dealer or look in one of the many aquarist magazines that are available to find information about clubs. These clubs will inform you – usually via a regular newsletter – of regional shows and exhibitions, and they can also provide you with up-to-the-minute expert advice on every aspect of modern fishkeeping.

TROPICAL FRESHWATER

62 TIGER BARB

(Barbus tetrazona) Barbs are undemanding and easy to feed. Although barbs are generally peaceful, Tiger Barbs tend to be fin-nippers, so avoid mixing them with angelfish.

Black dorsal fin has a red edge

CHARACTERISTICS
Size: 2½ in (6 cm)
Tank levels: Middle & lower
Temperament: Peaceful
Diet: Omnivorous

Body is crossed by four dark bands

63 ZEBRA DANIO

(Brachydanio rerio) Strikingly marked by bright blue or purple stripes, this species is highly active in the upper levels of the water. Selective breeding has produced both long-finned and veil-tailed varieties.

Upturned mouth adapted for surface feeding

CHARACTERISTICS
Size: 1¾ in (4.5 cm)
Tank levels: Upper
Temperament: Peaceful; schooling
Diet: Omnivorous

LONG-FINNED VARIETY

64 WHITE CLOUD MOUNTAIN MINNOW

(*Tanichthys albonubes*) A gold stripe, overlaid by blue lines, runs horizontally along the length of the body, where it terminates in a dark patch surrounded by a burst of red. This tiny, omnivorous fish is highly active in the upper levels of the tank. It is a prolific spawner, which makes it an excellent choice for first attempts at breeding fish.

Distinctive
gold stripe

Dark-edged scales

Red base of
caudal fin

CHARACTERISTICS
Size: 2 in (5 cm)
Tank levels: Upper
Temperament: Peaceful
Diet: Omnivorous

65 RED OSCAR

(*Astronotus ocellatus*)
This Red or Tiger Oscar is a popular pet despite its large size and voracious appetite. It will readily become hand-tame if fed from fingers. It requires regular, thorough water changes. Juvenile oscars have a marbled coloring.

Distinctive
red pigment

CHARACTERISTICS
Size: 11¼ in (28 cm)
Tank levels: Middle & lower
Temperament: Aggressive
Diet: Carnivorous

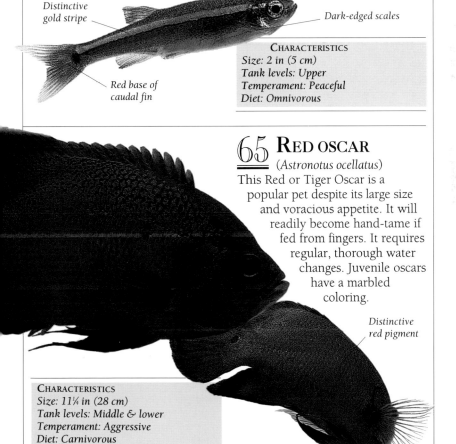

66 SIAMESE FIGHTING FISH

(*Betta splendens*) Despite its name, this species is not aggressive toward other species, and it makes an attractive addition to your tropical freshwater community aquarium. However, the males, which are easily distinguished by their spectacular fins, are aggressive toward other males of their own species, so keep only one per tank.

Long, flowing anal fin

Females have shorter fins

CHARACTERISTICS
Size: 2½ in (6 cm)
Tank levels: All
Temperament: Peaceful
Diet: Omnivorous

67 BLACK PHANTOM TETRA

(*Megalamphodus megalopterus*) As its common name suggests, this unusual fish has a wraithlike, transparent body displaying its internal organs. It has a distinctive dark spot on each shoulder. This lively fish is happiest in soft, acidic water.

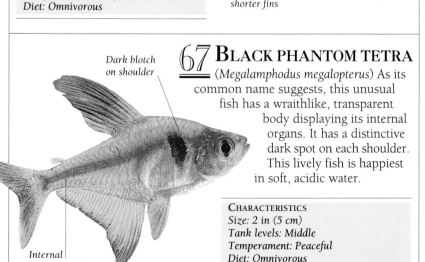

Dark blotch on shoulder

Internal organs visible

CHARACTERISTICS
Size: 2 in (5 cm)
Tank levels: Middle
Temperament: Peaceful
Diet: Omnivorous

Two black
bars on female
upper body

Female retains
yellow juvenile
coloration

68 AURATUS
(*Melanochromis auratus*) As
juveniles, both males and females
have a yellow coloration. Mature
males, however, have dark blue-
black bodies. This species is
intolerant of other fish. Keep
the male with a harem of females.

CHARACTERISTICS
Size: 5 in (13 cm)
Tank levels: Middle & lower
Temperament: Territorial
Diet: Herbivorous

69 ANGELFISH
(*Pterophyllum scalare*) With
their elegant, disklike shape, long
flowing fins, and graceful swimming
action, Angelfish are highly popular.
They are also favored for their
attentive parental care while
breeding; both parents
protect and fan water
over their eggs, which
are laid on leaves and
stems. Selective breeding
programs have produced a
wide variety of color strains. This
attractive species requires a deep
tank to develop fully.

Long, flowing
dorsal fin
with blunt tip
on juvenile

JUVENILE
ANGELFISH

CHARACTERISTICS
Size: 5 in (12.5 cm)
Tank levels: All
Temperament: Peaceful
Diet: Carnivorous

70 STRIATUM

(*Aphyosemion striatum*) This killifish has bright red horizontal lines across its body on an iridescent blue-green background. The lyre-shaped caudal fin has extended top and bottom rays. This species prefers a well-planted tank. Many killifish live for only a single season.

Two red lines on dorsal fin

Blue-green ring around eye

CHARACTERISTICS
Size: 2½ in (6 cm)
Tank levels: Upper
Temperament: Single-species tank
Diet: Carnivorous

Red-flecked anal fin

71 BEARDED CORYDORAS

(*Corydoras barbatus*) Like many catfish, this species is gregarious. It is covered with two distinctive rows of bony plates, or scutes. The whiskerlike growths, which give the catfish its name, are used for detecting food on riverbeds. This is a particularly active species.

Tall, tapering dorsal fin

Downturned mouth with two pairs of barbels

Reticular patterning

CHARACTERISTICS
Size: 3½ in (9 cm)
Tank levels: Lower
Temperament: Peaceful; schooling
Diet: Omnivorous

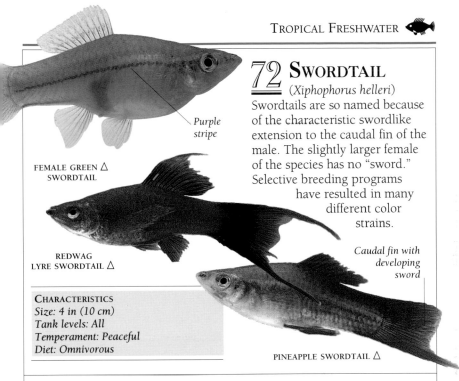

72 SWORDTAIL
(Xiphophorus helleri)
Swordtails are so named because of the characteristic swordlike extension to the caudal fin of the male. The slightly larger female of the species has no "sword." Selective breeding programs have resulted in many different color strains.

Purple stripe

FEMALE GREEN △
SWORDTAIL

REDWAG
LYRE SWORDTAIL △

Caudal fin with developing sword

PINEAPPLE SWORDTAIL △

CHARACTERISTICS
Size: 4 in (10 cm)
Tank levels: All
Temperament: Peaceful
Diet: Omnivorous

73 DWARF CHAINED LOACH
(Botia sidthimunki) A chain-link pattern across the length of its body gives this loach its common name. Shy, nocturnal creatures, loaches prefer a well-planted aquarium with plenty of retreats. They may need to be coaxed into view with their favorite worm-type food. This species has four pairs of barbels.

Four pairs of barbels

Caudal fin has black markings

CHARACTERISTICS
Size: 3 in (7.5 cm)
Tank levels: Lower
Temperament: Peaceful, schooling
Diet: Omnivorous

All fins, excluding the caudal fin, are clear

74 DISCUS

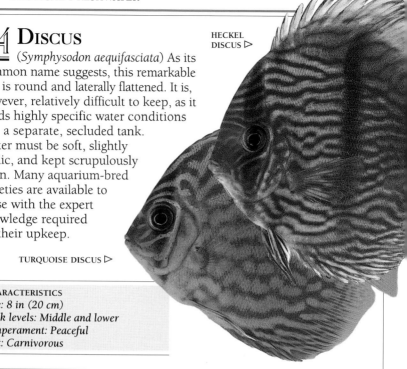

HECKEL DISCUS ▷

(*Symphysodon aequifasciata*) As its common name suggests, this remarkable fish is round and laterally flattened. It is, however, relatively difficult to keep, as it needs highly specific water conditions and a separate, secluded tank. Water must be soft, slightly acidic, and kept scrupulously clean. Many aquarium-bred varieties are available to those with the expert knowledge required for their upkeep.

TURQUOISE DISCUS ▷

CHARACTERISTICS
Size: 8 in (20 cm)
Tank levels: Middle and lower
Temperament: Peaceful
Diet: Carnivorous

75 GUPPY

(*Poecilia reticulata*) A hardy fish, the wild Guppy is dark olive green, but aquarium-bred varieties are also available in a wide range of colors. Males have more vibrant colors and more extravagant finnage than the females.

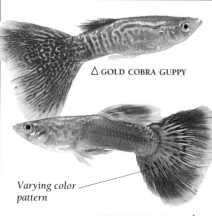

△ GOLD COBRA GUPPY

Varying color pattern

RED VARITAIL GUPPY △

CHARACTERISTICS
Size: 1¼ in (3 cm)
Tank levels: All
Temperament: Peaceful
Diet: Omnivorous

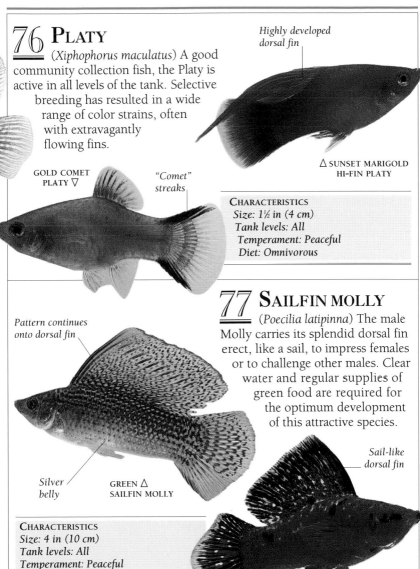

76 PLATY

(*Xiphophorus maculatus*) A good community collection fish, the Platy is active in all levels of the tank. Selective breeding has resulted in a wide range of color strains, often with extravagantly flowing fins.

Highly developed dorsal fin

△ SUNSET MARIGOLD HI-FIN PLATY

GOLD COMET PLATY ▽

"Comet" streaks

CHARACTERISTICS
Size: 1½ in (4 cm)
Tank levels: All
Temperament: Peaceful
Diet: Omnivorous

77 SAILFIN MOLLY

(*Poecilia latipinna*) The male Molly carries its splendid dorsal fin erect, like a sail, to impress females or to challenge other males. Clear water and regular supplies of green food are required for the optimum development of this attractive species.

Pattern continues onto dorsal fin

Sail-like dorsal fin

Silver belly

GREEN △ SAILFIN MOLLY

CHARACTERISTICS
Size: 4 in (10 cm)
Tank levels: All
Temperament: Peaceful
Diet: Omnivorous

△ STARBURST MOLLY

COLDWATER FRESHWATER

78 COMMON GOLDFISH

(*Carassius auratus*) Goldfish are divided into two distinct types: the hardy single-tail specimens, such as the Common Goldfish, and the more delicate, exotic-looking twin-tails, such as the Moor (*see p.59*). The Common Goldfish is usually metallic orange-red. Goldfish feed at every level of the tank, and accept most foods, but their diet should contain plenty of carbohydrates.

CHARACTERISTICS
.Size: Variable – up to 8 in (20 cm)
Tank levels: All
Temperament: Peaceful
Diet: Omnivorous

— *Reddish area behind gill cover*

79 RED SHINER

(*Notropis lutrensis*) This slim fish displays purple and blue body coloration with red fins and red markings on its head. Red Shiners thrive in a single-species tank. They require plenty of swimming space in well-oxygenated water.

CHARACTERISTICS
Size: Variable – up to 3 in (7.5 cm)
Tank levels: All
Temperament: Single-species tank
Diet: Omnivorous

△ GOLD RUDD

Shiny, well-defined scales

△ SILVER RUDD

Reddish fins

80 RUDD

(*Scardinius erythrophthalmus*) Both the wild Silver Rudd and the cultivated Gold Rudd need plenty of space in well-planted aquariums. The Rudd feeds at all tank levels. It can grow to over 8 in (20 in) long, so only juveniles should be kept in captivity. When it eventually outgrows its tank, it should be released into a pond. This species hybridizes readily with other similar species, such as the Roach, the Bleak, and the Silver Bream.

CHARACTERISTICS
Size: 20 cm (8 in)
Tank levels: All
Temperament: Schooling
Diet: Omnivorous

81 MOOR

(*Carassius auratus*) The Moor is actually an aquarium-bred twin-tailed goldfish. The coloration is always black, hence its alternative name, Black Moor. It has an egg-shaped body and, in some strains, protruding "telescopic" eyes. Any sign of silver is penalized at shows.

CHARACTERISTICS
Size: Variable – up to 8 in (20 cm)
Tank levels: All
Temperament: Peaceful
Diet: Omnivorous

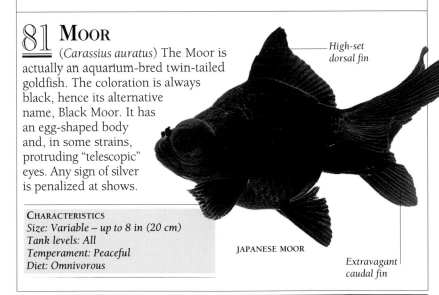

High-set dorsal fin

JAPANESE MOOR

Extravagant caudal fin

82 BUBBLE-EYE GOLDFISH

(*Carassius auratus*) The enlarged fluid-filled sacs beneath the eyes of this variety of twin-tailed Goldfish are highly distinctive, and they sway as the fish swims. These eye sacs are prone to damage, so it is advisable to keep this strain in its own tank. Avoid using sharp-edged furnishings when aquascaping.

Fluid-filled sac beneath eye

CHARACTERISTICS
Size: Variable – up to 8 in (20 cm)
Tank levels: All
Temperament: Peaceful
Diet: Omnivorous

Egg-shaped body with no dorsal fin

Red-orange coloration spreads into double caudal fin

83 SHUBUNKIN

(*Carassius auratus*) A variation of the Common Goldfish, the Shubunkin has a similarly rounded body. It is distinguished from the Common Goldfish by its opalescent scales, which may be a mixture of blue, purple, red, yellow, brown, orange, and black, depending on the strain. The strain shown here is the Bristol Shubunkin, with its distinctive rounded caudal fin.

Long-based dorsal fin

CHARACTERISTICS
Size: Variable – up to 8 in (20 in)
Tank levels: All
Temperament: Peaceful
Diet: Omnivorous

Mottled, opalescent coloration

84 CHINESE SAILFIN SUCKER

(*Myxocyprinus asiatica sinensis*) The beak-like profile of this ponderous fish is exaggerated by the tall dorsal fin and the fish's flat belly. The basic color of the original species is golden brown; the subspecies that is shown here is rust colored. Although it is often sold with tropical fish, this intriguing subspecies does not need tropical temperatures. It must be kept in a large, well-planted aquarium.

Three dark, vertical bands

CHARACTERISTICS
Size: 12 in (30 cm)
Tank levels: Lower
Temperament: Schooling
Diet: Omnivorous

Distinctive two-tone coloration

85 RED & WHITE RYUKIN

(*Carassius auratus*) Like the Moor (*see p.59*), this elegant fish is a strain of twin-tailed Goldfish. It has the same egg-shaped body as the Moor, but it has a two-tone coloration. Like all twin-tailed Goldfish, it is relatively slow and delicate. It is not suitable for outdoor ponds, where its delicate, flowing fins might be damaged.

Elegant, double caudal fin

CHARACTERISTICS
Size: Variable – up to 8 in (20 cm)
Tank levels: All
Temperament: Peaceful
Diet: Omnivorous

TROPICAL MARINE

86 FLAME ANGELFISH

(*Centropyge loriculus*) A good species for the novice tropical marine fishkeeper, the Flame Angelfish is hardy and relatively easy to manage. It can be territorial, so keep it with larger fish.

Intense, flame orange body

CHARACTERISTICS
Size: 4 in (10 cm)
Tank levels: Lower
Temperament: Peaceful
Diet: Omnivorous

Four or five dark bands across body

87 JEWEL MORAY EEL

(*Muraena lentiginosa*) Not for the beginner, this carnivorous eel is territorial and its jaws are powerful and filled with sharp teeth. It can be kept as a specimen fish in a spacious aquarium with other large fishes. It is a sea-cave dweller, so provide a suitable retreat.

CHARACTERISTICS
Size: 24 in (60 cm)
Tank levels: Lower
Temperament: Territorial & aggressive
Diet: Carnivorous

Powerful, tooth-filled jaws

88 DOMINO DAMSELFISH

(*Dascyllus trimaculatus*) Relatively inexpensive and easy to keep, this species is popular with beginners. Three spots on the body give it a domino-like appearance. The white spots diminish with age, and the rich black coloration fades to gray if the fish is unhappy with its tank conditions. Provide plenty of retreats and finely chopped meaty food.

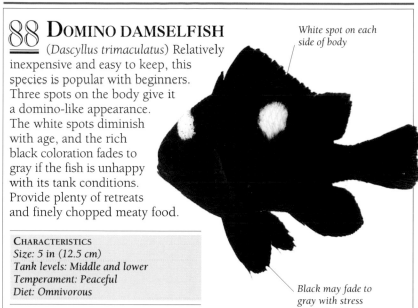

White spot on each side of body

Black may fade to gray with stress

CHARACTERISTICS
Size: 5 in (12.5 cm)
Tank levels: Middle and lower
Temperament: Peaceful
Diet: Omnivorous

89 COMMON CLOWNFISH

(*Amphiprion ocellaris*) Clownfish may have acquired their name from their comical, waddling swimming action. Provide this species with a sea anemone – its natural sanctuary in its coral reef habitat. This fish can be territorial.

Black-edged white bands

CHARACTERISTICS
Size: 2¼ in (7 cm)
Tank levels: Middle and lower
Temperament: Peaceful; territorial
Diet: Omnivorous

90 COPPERBANDED BUTTERFLYFISH

(*Chelmon rostratus*) All butterflyfish share the stunning coloration of their relatives the angelfish. This fish displays deep orange bands with a false eye-spot to distract predators. Its long snout is ideal for picking food out of corals. It is difficult to maintain in captivity.

Black-edged
orange bands

CHARACTERISTICS
Size: 7 in (18 cm)
Tank levels: Middle and lower
Temperament: Aggressive
Diet: Carnivorous

Long snout for
picking out food

91 FIREFISH

(*Nemateleotris magnifica*) The coloration of this species is divided into two distinct areas: the front half of the body is pinkish yellow with speckling on the head, while the rear is pinkish orange, shading through to a dark red-brown. Retreats are essential – this species naturally inhabits reef caves.

CHARACTERISTICS
Size: 2½ in (6 cm)
Tank levels: Middle and lower
Temperament: Single species tank
Diet: Carnivorous

Elongated first
ray of dorsal fin

Reddish
brown
caudal fin

Long pelvic fins
anchor fish to
resting place

92 CROWNED SQUIRRELFISH

(*Holocentrus diadema*)
Squirrelfish are nocturnal; they patrol the aquarium in schools at night but generally hide in retreats during the day. This large species is distinguished by rows of thin white lines across its bright red body. Squirrelfish make sounds by grinding their teeth together. This is thought to be a means of communication.

Large eyes typical of family

Red edges to anal, caudal, and pectoral fins

CHARACTERISTICS
Size: 12 in (30 cm)
Tank levels: Lower
Temperament: Aggressive; schooling
Diet: Carnivorous

93 YELLOW TANG

(*Zebrasoma flavescens*) This brilliant yellow species has a sloping forehead and long snout. Although relatively easy to keep, it should not be introduced into an aquarium until a good deal of algae has grown. It should be fed regularly on green foods.

Retractable spine used as defense mechanism

Steeply sloping forehead and high-set eyes

CHARACTERISTICS
Size: 8 in (20 cm)
Tank levels: All
Temperament: Territorial
Diet: Herbivorous

Uniformly yellow fins

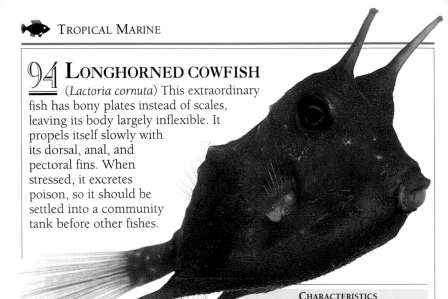

94 LONGHORNED COWFISH

(*Lactoria cornuta*) This extraordinary fish has bony plates instead of scales, leaving its body largely inflexible. It propels itself slowly with its dorsal, anal, and pectoral fins. When stressed, it excretes poison, so it should be settled into a community tank before other fishes.

Tapering box-shaped body

CHARACTERISTICS
Size: 20 in (50 cm)
Tank levels: Lower
Temperament: Shy
Diet: Omnivorous

95 MANDARINFISH

(*Synchiropus splendidus*) A bottom-dwelling fish, the Mandarinfish is extremely shy. Its body is a bluish green-gold, with a random pattern of blue lines to provide good camouflage in coral reefs. Keep the Mandarinfish in a quiet tank, away from more boisterous fish.

CHARACTERISTICS
Size: 3 in (7.5 cm)
Tank levels: Lower
Temperament: Shy
Diet: Carnivorous

Bright blue rim on dorsal fin

96 CUBAN HOGFISH

(Bodianus puchellus) A member of the Wrasse family, these fish have intriguing behavior patterns, including sex reversal in single-sexed groups, and the building of nighttime "cocoons." Juveniles clean parasites from other fish.

CHARACTERISTICS
Size: 10 in (25 cm)
Tank levels: All
Temperament: Peaceful
Diet: Carnivorous

Long-based
dorsal fin

Tapering
white band
on adult

97 TAILBAR LIONFISH

(Pterois radiata) Decidedly unsuitable for beginners, the deep reddish brown, stocky body of this formidable fish bristles with spiny, venomous fin rays. Its graceful swimming action belies its stealthy, predatory instinct. It lies in wait for its prey, which it then engulfs in its large mouth. Handle lionfish with extreme caution.

CHARACTERISTICS
Size: 10 in (25 cm)
Tank levels: All
Temperament: Aggressive
Diet: Carnivorous

Horny extensions
above eyes

COLDWATER MARINE

98 GUNNEL

(*Pholis gunnellus*) An eellike fish, the golden brown Gunnel has contrasting vertical bands that disappear as it matures. Dark spots appear along the dorsal fin. Provide plenty of retreats and meaty foods.

CHARACTERISTICS
Size: 10 in (25 cm)
Tank levels: Lower
Temperament: Single-species tank
Diet: Carnivorous

Dark spots with pale rims along dorsal fin

99 LEOPARD-SPOTTED GOBY

(*Thorogobius ephippiatus*) The reddish brown blotches on its creamy yellow body give this fish its common name. It has a blunt head with a large mouth and high-set eyes. It is extremely timid and requires plenty of suitable hideaways.

CHARACTERISTICS
Size: 5 in (12.5 cm)
Tank levels: Lower
Temperament: Shy
Diet: Omnivorous

Broad, blunt head with high-set eyes

100 FIFTEEN-SPINED STICKLEBACK

(*Spinachia spinachia*) The 15 spines that give this brownish fish its name are the remnants of the spiny front of the dorsal fin. Its body tapers dramatically toward its caudal fin. All sticklebacks require small live foods in their diet.

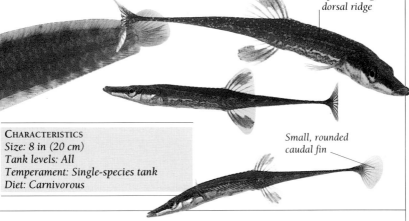

Spines along dorsal ridge

Small, rounded caudal fin

CHARACTERISTICS
Size: 8 in (20 cm)
Tank levels: All
Temperament: Single-species tank
Diet: Carnivorous

101 YARRELL'S BLENNY

(*Chirolophis ascanii*) This species can be identified by the characteristic growths above its eyes. Blennies are active fish that scuttle around the base of the tank. Although territorial and likely to harass smaller fish, Yarrell's Blenny may itself be intimidated by larger fish. It needs rocky retreats and feeds mainly on meaty foods.

CHARACTERISTICS
Size: 10 in (25 cm)
Tank levels: Lower
Temperament: Territorial; aggressive
Diet: Omnivorous

Branched tentacle above each eye

Large mouth with relatively thick lips

INDEX

A

aeration, 26
ailments, 49
air pumps, 26
algae, 37, 47
Angelfish, 53
  Emperor, 21
  Flame, 12, 62
  French, 18
Anostomus, Striped, 10
Anubias, 36, 39
aquascaping, 30–9
artificial plants, 37
Auratus, 53

B

bamboo plant, 36
base coverings, 30, 32
biological filtration, 26, 34
Bitterling, 11
Blenny:
  Tompot, 9
  Yarrell's, 69
Butterflyfish,
  Copperbanded, 64

C

catching fish, 46
Catfish, 21
Chinese Sailfin Sucker, 61
Cichlid, Lemon, 28
cleaning tanks, 31, 47
Clown Knife Fish, 43
Clownfish, Common, 63
Clubs, 49
coldwater fish:
  freshwater, 11, 58–61
  marine, 13, 68–9
Comet, 11
compatible fish, 19
Corydoras, Bearded, 54
Cowfish, Longhorned, 66

D

Damselfish, Domino, 63
dealers, 14, 17
Discus Fish, 56
diseases, 17, 49

E

Eel, Blue Ribbon, 19
eel grass, 36
equipment, 22–9, 31

F

feeding, 40–3
filters, 22, 25–6
  aquascaping, 34
  biological, 26
  cleaning, 47
fin-nipping, 44
Firefish, 64
flake food, 41
freshwater fish, 9
  coldwater, 11, 58–61
  tropical, 10, 50–7
frozen foods, 41

G

Goby, Leopard-spotted, 68
Goldfish, 21
  Bubble-eye, 15, 60
  Common, 11, 18, 58
  Fantail, 11
Gourami, 10
Grouper, Polka Dot, 12
Gularis, Blue, 9
Gunnel, 68
Guppy, 56

H

heaters, 10, 22, 27
Hogfish, Cuban, 67
hospital tanks, 49
Humbug, Black-tailed, 19
Hygrophila, Giant, 36

J

Java Fern, 39
jetlagged stock, 17

K

Killifish, 21
Koi, 21

L

lifespan, 21
lighting, 22, 29
Lionfish, Tailbar, 67
live food, 42
Loach:
  Clown, 44
  Dwarf Chained, 55
  Zebra, 35

M

Mandarinfish, 66
marine fish, 9, 13
  aquascaping, 37
  changing water, 48

coldwater, 13, 68–9
tropical, 12, 62–7
Minnow, White Cloud
  Mountain, 51
Molly, Sailfin, 57
Moor, 59
Moray Eel, Jewel, 62
mouths, 20
Mullet, 13

N

netting, 46
new fish, introducing, 45

O

observation, 44
Oranda, Red-Cap, 11
Oscar, Red, 51
overfeeding, 43
oxygen, 11, 23, 26

P

Paradise Fish, 10
parasites, 49
Piranha, Red-bellied, 18
plants, 30–1, 35–9, 47
Platy, 57
  Sunset Marigold Hi-Fin,
  10
poisoning, 46
prepacked food, 41
Pufferfish, Black-Saddled, 9
pumps, 22, 26

Q

quarantine, 49

R

Ram, 28
Rasbora:
  Harlequin, 15
  Red-Striped, 19

Rock Cock, 13
rocks, 33
Rotala, Giant Red, 36
Royal Gramma, 12
Rudd, 59
Ryukin, Red and White,
  61

S

sea anemones, 12, 37
Sea Horse, 15
"sea mix", 28, 48
Sea Scorpion,
  Long-Spined, 13
seaweed, artificial, 37
Shiner, Red, 58
Shubunkin, 9, 60
Siamese Fighting Fish, 10,
  52
size of fish, 18
Squirrelfish, Crowned, 65
Stickleback, Fifteen-
  Spined, 13, 69
stocking levels, 23
stress, 45, 48
Striatum, 54
swim-bladder disorders, 49
Swordtail, 55

T

Tang, Yellow, 65
tanks:
  aeration, 26
  base coverings,
  32
  cleaning, 31,
  47
  filters, 25–6
  heaters, 10, 22,
  27
  lighting, 29
  quarantine, 49

shape, 24
siting, 24
stocking levels, 23
Tetra, 21
  Black Phantom, 52
  Silver Dollar, 35
thermometers, 27
Tiger Barb, 8, 10, 50
travel, 48
tropical fish:
  freshwater, 10, 50–7
  marine, 12, 62–7

V

Vacation feeding, 43
Vallis, Twisted, 38–9
vets, 49

W

water, 28
  changing, 48
Waterweed, 36
Wisteria, Water, 39
worms, 42
Wrasse, Twinspot, 44

Z

Zebra Danio, 50

ACKNOWLEDGMENTS

Dorling Kindersley would like to thank Hilary Bird for compiling the index and Ann Kay for proofreading. Thanks also to Chenies Aquatics at Kennedy's Garden Center, Slough, England, for the loan of equipment.

Photography
KEY: t *top*; b *bottom*; c *center*; l *left*; r *right*
All photographs by Jerry Young except:
Paul Bricknell 8b, 11br, 22, 23, 31br, 33bl, 36bl, bc, br, 41t, bl, 42tr, b, 43b, 46, 47, 48, 49t; Max Gibbs 10bl, 16, 25tr, 40b, 44b; Jane Burton, Kim Taylor 2, 6c, b, 8t, 10bl, br, 11bl, 13 br, 20b, 24b, 27bl, 28b, 30, 31b, 32, 33t, c, br, 34, 35t, 36t, 37, 38, 39, 41c, br, 42l, c, 45, 49b, 67t, 68t; Max Gibbs 10bl, 16, 25tr, 40b, 44b; Dave King 18br, 21b, 29b, 44t, 71; Dick Mills 9tl, 60b; David Sands 8c; Matthew Ward 25c, 26b, 27br, 29tl, tr; The Goldfish Bowl 1, 6t, 14t, 19c, 21t

Illustrations
Linden Artists Ltd (Stewart Lafford) 23, 24
Janos Marffy 40